This
belongs to

....

make
believe
ideas

Cinderella

Key sound ow spellings: ow, ou
Secondary sounds: th, ll, wh

Written by Nick Page
Illustrated by Clare Fennell

Reading with phonics

How to use this book

The **Reading with phonics** series helps you to have fun with your child and to support their learning of phonics and reading. It is aimed at children who have learned the letter sounds and are building confidence in their reading.

Each title in the series focuses on a different key sound. The entertaining retelling of the story repeats this sound frequently, and the different spellings for the sound are highlighted in red type. The first activity at the back of the book provides practice in reading and using words that contain this sound. The key sound for **Cinderella** is **ow**.

Start by reading the story to your child, asking them to join in with the refrain in bold. Next, encourage them to read the story with you. Give them a hand to decode tricky words.

Now look at the activity pages at the back of the book. These are intended for you and your child to enjoy together. Most are not activities to complete in pencil or pen, but by reading and talking or pointing.

The **Key sound** pages focus on one sound, and on the various different groups of letters that produce that sound. Encourage your child to read the different letter groups and complete the activity, so they become more aware of the variety of spellings there are for the same sound.

The **Letters together** pages look at three pairs or groups of letters and at the sounds they make as they work together. Help your child to read the words and trace the route on the word maps.

Rhyme is used a lot in these retellings. Whatever stage your child has reached in their learning of phonics, it is always good practice for them to listen carefully for sounds and spot words that rhyme. The pages on **Rhyming words** take six words from the story and ask children to read and spot other words that rhyme with them.

The **Key words** pages focus on a number of key words that occur regularly but can nonetheless be tricky. Many of these words are not sounded out following the rules of phonics and the easiest thing is for children to learn them by sight, so that they do not worry about decoding them. These pages encourage children to retell the story, practising key words as they do so.

The **Picture dictionary** page asks children to focus closely on nine words from the story. Encourage children to look carefully at each word, cover it with their hand, write it on a separate piece of paper, and finally, check it!

Do not complete all the activities at once – doing one each time you read will ensure that your child continues to enjoy the stories and the time you are spending together. **Have fun!**

"Cinderella, clean the house!"
"Cinderella, wash my blouse!"
"Cinderella, you behave!"
"Cinderella, you're a slave!"
Every day, they'd howl and shout
and order the poor girl about.

4

The magic wand spins round and round.
Will Cinderella's prince be found?

5

Wicked stepmum makes
her clean,

two stepsisters are so mean.

Not allowed a nice, warm bed,
she sleeps by the fire instead,
near the ashes, in the cellar,
so they call her Cinderella.

The magic wand spins round and round.
Will Cinderella's prince be found?

An announcement to the town:

"Every girl, put on your gown,

it's the party of your life!

The prince is scouting for a wife!"

"What shall I wear?" Cinders asks.

"You can't go! Back to your tasks!"

The magic wand spins round and round.
Will Cinderella's prince be found?

As the others head to town,
Cinders cries. She's feeling down.

When – POW! – a fairy dame appears.
"You shall go to the ball, my dear!
Your fairy godmother has arrived –
now dry your eyes and get outside."

**The magic wand spins round and round.
Will Cinderella's prince be found?**

She waves her wand – round and round,
and Cinders has a lovely gown,
a magic carriage made of gold,
and two glass shoes (they're very cold).

"Be home before
the midnight hour,
or else this spell
will lose its power."

The magic wand spins round and round.
Will Cinderella's prince be found?

13

Dong! Dong!

At the ball, the crowd's amazed,
the prince is wowed – completely dazed.
And all that night, this charming fella
dances just with Cinderella.
Until the clock bells in the tower
start to chime the midnight hour!
The magic wand spins round and round.
Will Cinderella's prince be found?

15

"It's midnight now! I must get out!
I've got to go! Can't wait about!"
And as the spell starts losing power,
she runs at ninety miles an hour!

On the steps, she leaves behind
a glass shoe for the prince to find.

**The magic wand spins
round and round.
Will Cinderella's
prince be found?**

Around the town Prince Charming goes,
fitting the glass shoe on the toes
of every girl, even her sisters.
(They vow it fits, despite the blisters.)

"Try me!" A sound comes from the cellar.
"Pipe down," shouts Mum to Cinderella.

Try me!

The magic wand spins round and round.
Will Cinderella's prince be found?

"You know you're not allowed upstairs!"

"No! Bring her out!" the prince declares.

The glass shoe fits her perfectly.

Her stepmum cries, "It cannot be!"

But Cinders has the other shoe!

The prince says,

"Take a bow – it's you!"

Perfect!

The magic wand spins round and round.
Will Cinderella's prince be found?

Bells are ringing – hear the sound
of happy endings all around.
Cinders and the prince are wed;
he sets a crown upon her head.
Everyone is so delighted!
(But not Stepmum – she's not invited!)

The magic wand spins round and round.
Cinderella's prince is found!

Key sound

There are different groups of letters that make the **ow** sound. Practise them by looking at the words in Cinderella's gowns and using them to make sentences. Can you use each word in a different sentence?

house

blouse   sound

about

shout

round

around

outside

announce

clown

frown

town

crown

gown

crowd

allowed

power

tower

Letters together

Look at these pairs of letters and say
the sounds they make.

th **ll** **wh**

Follow the words that contain **th** to
help Cinderella find her godmother.

th

the

shout they

this

slave

clean other

godmothe

fire

cellar

Follow the words that contain **ll** to ring the wedding bells for Cinderella.

ll

cellar — shoe

prince — crown

spell — wife — party

bells — lots — other

Follow the words that contain **wh** to help Cinderella find her white dress.

what — **wh**

when

why — slipper

other

clean — white

where

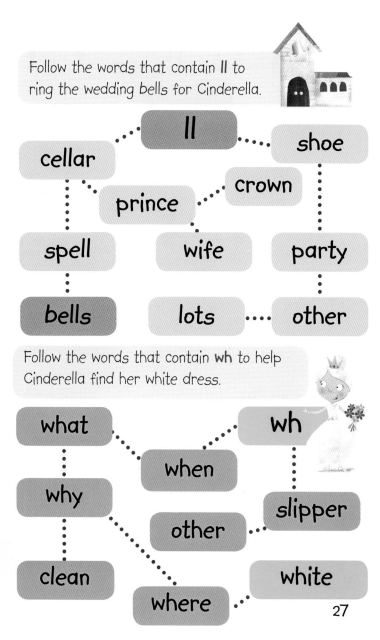

Rhyming words

Read the words in the flowers
and point to other words that
rhyme with them.

prince	**gown**	down
shoes		crown

clean	**clock**	shock
knock		dance

house	**spell**	tell
fell		blouse

ball	dance	chance
prance		bells

mince	prince	slave
since		shout

steps	gold	cold
sold		cellar

Now choose a word and make up a rhyming chant!

I wear a **crown** and a **gown** as I spin **round** and **round**.

29

Key words

Many common words can be tricky to sound out. Practise them by reading these sentences about the story. Now make more sentences using other key words from around the border.

Cinderella and the prince danced **and** danced.

The fairy **made** shoes and a gown for Cinderella.

The prince tried the shoe on **every** girl.

There was an invitation **from** the prince!

Cinderella went **to** the ball.

to · there's · every · cold · ever · across · from · a

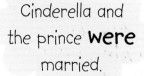

Cinderella worked **as** a slave.

Cinderella and the prince **were** married.

The sisters **told** Cinderella she couldn't go to the ball.

The stepsisters' feet **didn't** fit the shoe.

Cinderella left her shoe **on** the steps.

not • had • look • little • there • were • asked • fell • really • better • once •

• this • dog • didn't • told • going • made • and • they •

Picture dictionary

Look carefully at the pictures and the words.
Now cover the words, one at a time.
Can you remember how to write them?

bell   carriage   clock

crown   fire   gold

gown   shoe   toes

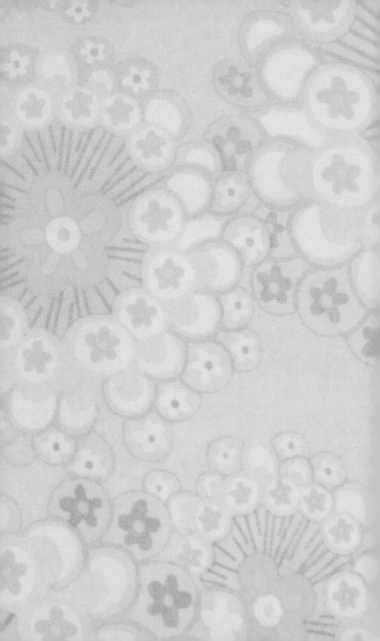